# THE INSIDER SECRET OF
# BUSINESS

# THE INSIDER SECRET OF BUSINESS

## Growing Successful Financially and Productively

ALAIN IMPONGE

authorHOUSE®

*AuthorHouse™ UK*
*1663 Liberty Drive*
*Bloomington, IN 47403 USA*
*www.authorhouse.co.uk*
*Phone: 0800.197.4150*

© 2014 Alain Imponge. All rights reserved.

*No part of this book may be reproduced, stored in a retrieval system, or transmitted by any means without the written permission of the author.*

*Published by AuthorHouse 07/25/2015*

*ISBN: 978-1-4969-9966-5 (sc)*
*ISBN: 978-1-4969-9965-8 (hc)*
*ISBN: 978-1-4969-9967-2 (e)*

*Print information available on the last page.*

*Any people depicted in stock imagery provided by Thinkstock are models, and such images are being used for illustrative purposes only. Certain stock imagery © Thinkstock.*

*This book is printed on acid-free paper.*

*Because of the dynamic nature of the Internet, any web addresses or links contained in this book may have changed since publication and may no longer be valid. The views expressed in this work are solely those of the author and do not necessarily reflect the views of the publisher, and the publisher hereby disclaims any responsibility for them.*

# Contents

1  Planning: The Early Stages . . . . . . . . . . . . . 1

2  Premises . . . . . . . . . . . . . . . . . . . . . . . . 17

3  Financing . . . . . . . . . . . . . . . . . . . . . . . 23

4  Grants . . . . . . . . . . . . . . . . . . . . . . . . . 37

5  Starting an Import or Export Business (International Trading) . . . . . . . . . . . . . . . 61

6  Marketing . . . . . . . . . . . . . . . . . . . . . . . 75

# Planning: The Early Stages 1

Starting your own business can be one of the most rewarding ventures you ever undertake, but planning and research are vital if you want to improve your chances of making it a success. A good business idea is essential, but so too is a well-constructed business plan, knowledge of your market, and awareness of the legal issues. This book will take you step by step through all the necessary phases of starting up your own business, from the crucial planning stages to obtaining financing to advertising your services and product.

## Doing Your Research

Making the leap from employee to entrepreneur is exhilarating but also stressful. Basic research and planning are vital if you don't want your business to fall at the first hurdle. You must ask yourself, what makes you think your business will succeed? Is there a need for the product or service you hope to supply? What piece can the market support, and is that market growing or declining?

Use the Internet, the local library, and friends to research your intended market. Is there a gap in the market you could fill? What's your unique selling point (USP)? Consider how your business will be different from the competition. Not all businesses are based on entirely new ideas, but it's important to have a USP in mind – maybe a hard-to-beat service based on your experience and contacts or a low-priced service thanks to your great supply contact.

Finally, take an honest look at your own abilities. Not everyone is cut out to run a business. You'll need to work long hours and deal with lots of setbacks, all of which may affect your financial stability. This is a fact of life for most entrepreneurs. Will you be able to cope?

## The Business Plan

A business plan is a document that spells out exactly what your business will do and how it will make money. You'll need to show a business plan to your bank manager when applying for financial assistance, and it may also be useful when talking to potential partners, investors, and employees. It needn't be complex. As a rule of thumb, a good business plan should include:

- an overview of what your business will do, starting with why you think there is a market for your product or service and how you intend to make a profit.

- a financial forecast showing intended cash flow over a reasonable period of time. This should include predictions of total sales, costs associated with running the business, outside investment, and when you expect to move from break-even to profitability.

- an analysis of the competition. What other companies offer similar goods and services? What threats and challenges need to be overcome? How will you manage the risk associated with your new business venture?

- a description of your experience and qualifications together with those of your partners and senior employees, if appropriate. You should provide information on the track record and experience of all the people who will help your business on its way.

It's best to be as conservative as you can at this stage as you estimate what finances the company needs and where the money will come from.

## Legal Considerations

When you set up a business, you immediately take on a whole set of legal obligations and responsibilities that are designed to protect you and your employees, customers, and suppliers. There are many laws that govern how legally formed companies can act, such as the Trader Description Act and Sale of Goods Act, both of which have been put in place to protect the customer but also you as a supplier. Are you familiar with these laws and the obligations they place you under? Your solicitor will be able to fill you in on what's required.

### Type of Business

The first issue that needs to be decided is what sort of organisation you are setting up. Will you be a sole trader, partnership, or limited company?

Each sort of business has its own requirement, and you may need to register as an incorporated company.

- *Sole trader* is a term used to describe the simplest form of business entity, owned by one person. This type of entity is *unincorporated*, which means that in the eyes of the law, there is no distinction made between the business and its owner.

- *Partnerships* are business entities owned by two or more persons who carry on a business together with the intention of making a profit. As with sole traders, a partnership is an unincorporated business, and partners are personally liable for any action or inaction of the business.

- *Limited companies* are owned by individuals known as *shareholders*. Such business organisations are *incorporated*, meaning that each company has its own legal identity separate from that of its owners. In the eyes of the law, the limited company is a living person; it may enter into contracts in its own name and sue or be sued. Limited companies are divided into the following two groups:

  - *Private limited company*: This type of company, which must end its registered name with the word *limited* or the abbreviation *Ltd*, cannot offer its shares for sale to the general public, which tends to restrict the amount it is able to raise. This can be determined by its directors and can be less than £50,000.

- *Public limited company*: This type of company must end its name with the words *public limited company* or the abbreviation *plc* and must formally register as a public limited company. It is a legal requirement that public limited companies have authorised share capital of at least £50,000 (or the equivalent in euros).

**Business Name**

Your business name should be memorable and sum up what you do. It's important to register the name legally so that other companies can't use your business name in the future. There are also rules about what you can name a business; it can't be offensive or illegal. It's possible to check what company names are currently in use on the Companies House website at www.companieshouse.gov.uk.

If your business relies on a unique product or name, you should also think about trademarks, copyrights, and patents. A *trademark* protects a name and prevents others from using or abusing it. *Copyrights* and *patents* are there to stop the fruits of your labour from being used without your permission. Remember that you have to specifically apply for a patent.

**Insurance**

Insurance is also going to be a key issue. This usually splits into what you must take out by law and what's prudent to take out to adequately cover yourself – everything from employer's liability insurance to premises to specialist insurance for certain types of equipment and tools.

**Tax and National Insurance**

Last and very much not least, there are strict laws about how businesses should handle their finances. A good accountant will advise you on what your tax and National Insurance liabilities will be, although there is plenty of advice available from the Inland Revenue. There are strict financial penalties for poor filing and record-keeping, so it may be worth investing in special software to help you keep accurate tax and National Insurance records. Some packages will also help you file your tax returns online, which can save small businesses a lot of money. If you employ others, you will need to deal with PAYE and National Insurance, but it is likely you'll hire an accountant to handle these issues, as well as payroll.

## Keeping Business and Financial Information Secure

As a business owner, you will need to keep a scrupulous record of all your financial dealings as a purchaser and supplier from the outset; this is expected of all business and may be requested by the authorities. All business information should be kept secure and yet be filed in a system that makes it easily accessible to those authorised to use it. Simple security measures – such as keeping office doors locked when an office is unoccupied, locking filing cabinets, or keeping information in a lockable drawer or safe – should be encouraged.

Computer files should be protected with passwords and PINs to restrict access. Confidential information should be stored on removable files (tapes, discs or CDs) and kept in secure locations. The Data Protection Act requires that personal data be kept under safe and secure conditions. This would require the use of firewalls to protect the information from contamination or hackers.

Various filing systems are used in practice. These keep the financial information under safe and secure conditions whilst still allowing it to be easily retrievable. These include the following:

- filing in numerical order,

- filing in alphabetical order,

- filing in chronological (date) order

- filling geographically

# Premises 2

What sort of premises will you need for your business? Working from home can be attractive – the box room or garden shed is cheap and lets you put in extra hours when the business needs it – but working from home can be inconvenient for your family and may look unprofessional to potential customers.

If you decide to use a commercial business premises, there is a range of options, from full-service open-plan offices to high-street shops. Which you choose depends on the type of business you're starting. Some businesses, such as retail or manufacturing, can only take place in premises that are approved for this use. Check with your local council for details of planning regulations. As a rule of thumb, offices are classed as B1 premises, industrial units are B2, and warehouses are B8.

When deciding on a premises, keep the following factors in mind:

- *Locale.* Will you rely on passing trade on the high street, or is it important to be near an airport or motorway?

- *Space.* In an office, expect to provide 150 square feet per person, but remember you may also need private offices or meeting rooms. Consider whether you need room to store stock or paperwork.

- *Cost.* Serviced offices may look professional but could be expensive, while offices in less desirable areas of town will often be cheaper.

- *Facilities.* If you need special computer cabling or ventilation, this needs to be planned for in advance. Will you have lots of employees who need to park their cars?

## Renting or Leasing

It's usual for new businesses to rent rather than buy their premises. You should expect to sign a one-, three-, or six-month rental agreement (sometimes called a license) at minimum and pay for phone bills and other services on top of that. It's usual to pay monthly with a deposit of several months' rent for security.

A lease is more formal way of renting premises and can last for up to five years, with the monthly payment increasing by a set percentage each year. Leases are normally paid quarterly, and you may be expected to provide a large security deposit. In addition, tenants may be expected to pay for repairs and upkeep of the building, so it's worth taking the advice of a special solicitor before signing a lease agreement.

# Financing 3

Managing cash flow is the biggest financial challenge many young businesses face. However, keeping track of invoicing, bills, and day-to-day expenses are all essential elements of being your own boss. To remain solvent, you must effectively manage your cash flow. This basically means making sure that the money coming into your business each month (through sales, investment capital, or rent income) is greater than the money leaving the business (through routine payments such as rent, payroll and supplier payments).

If you find this difficult, there are dozens of software packages available to help monitor cash flow and forecast future finances. Many packages will help to calculate tax, VAT, and National Insurance payments based on your cash-flow calculations.

## Raising Financing for Your Business

Raising financing is a vital stage in the setting up, expansion, and day-to-day running of a business. Unless you are able to meet capital needs from personal resources – perhaps by using your savings, re-mortgaging a property, or borrowing from friends or family – you will need to turn to sources of external finance. The main categories of external finance are debt finance, equity finance, and asset finance. A range of grants and funds may also be available to smaller businesses.

**What Are Your Finance Requirements?**

A useful distinction can be made between start-up and working capital. Start-up capital is the money you need to get your business up and running. Necessary expenditures might include the following:

- premises
- plant and machinery
- office equipment
- legal and accountancy
- insurance
- stationery
- launch publicity

Working capital is the money needed to cover the interval between paying your suppliers and receiving payments from your own customers. There may be a considerable time lag during which you will have to continue paying materials, labour, and overhead.

Finance requirements vary according to the type of enterprise. A service business may require less start-up capital than a manufacturing enterprise because it needs little in the way of plant and equipment. But the service may face a long delay before receipts come in and need more working capital to bridge the gap. In some cases, financing may be required to buy an existing business or to support a management buyout or buy in.

**Forecasting**

To assess your financing needs, you will have to make a realistic estimate of the cost that will be involved in the acquisition, setting up, and running of your business. Running cost can be separated into *fixed costs*, which are incurred regardless of output or sales, and *variable costs*, which are determined by the performance of the business.

Potential lenders or investors will expect to see a business plan that includes financial forecasts. Draw up a profit-and-loss forecast for at least twelve months ahead, showing when you expect to break even, along with a cash-flow forecast that shows when you expect money to flow into and out of the business. It may be worthwhile to hire an accountant to help with the preparation of your financial forecasts.

Your business plan should set out the nature of your business and your credentials. Analyse the market in which you plan to operate, and outline how you will promote the business. You will need to explain what type of lending or investment you are seeking and give an account of your resources and liabilities.

## Banking

Most small business find it easier to keep track of their finances by using a business bank account, available from any high-street bank. If you have access to a computer, it's a good idea to look for a bank that also offers secure online banking facilities so you don't waste hours queuing up in branches to complete routine transaction

Banks offer all sorts of different packages for small businesses, so look carefully at charges for things like cheques, statements, and using cash machines. It's also worth asking if your bank offers free telephone or face to face advice for small businesses - many banks offer this for free to business customers.

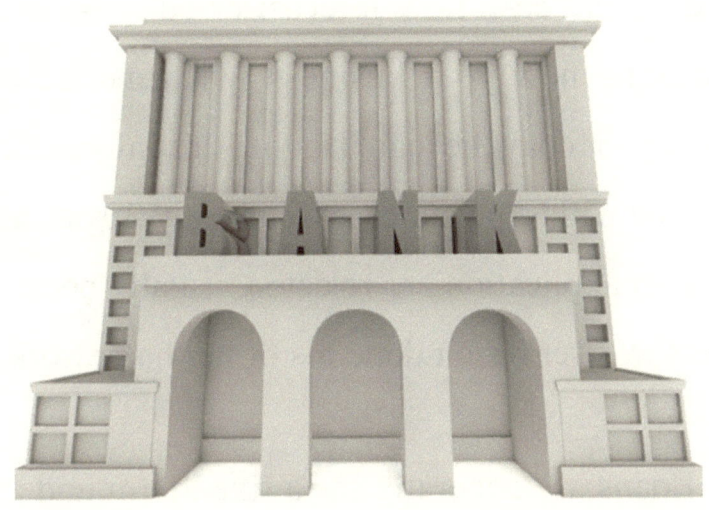

**Bank Loans**

Every business needs money to get started – this is often referred to as *seed capital* because it helps your business grow. A common source of funding for new businesses is a bank loan. High-street banks are the main source, although investment banks may make loans to large businesses.

When you apply for a loan, your bank will want to see recent tax returns, financial statements, and a solid cash-flow forecast or business plan, outlining how your business will generate the money to repay the loan. Having this information to hand will help your case – currently, 10 per cent of loan application are rejected, usually because the borrower hasn't done his or her homework.

Loans are generally for a fixed term and are repaid in monthly instalments. The interest rate, which may be available or fixed, will typically be set at a margin of 2 to 6 per cent above the base rate. There may be an arrangement fee of about 1 per cent of the amount of the loan. Mortgages are longer-term loans, usually for a twenty-five year period.

Most high-street banks have a specialist unit that deals with business customers, and it may offer special deals with features such as repayment holidays. It is best to shop around and compare what a number of potential lenders have on offer. Make sure that you have a clear understanding of the charges, terms, and conditions of any loan, as you will be committing to a long-term arrangement.

Banks will expect to see a long-term plan for your business, including financial forecast and regular information about the performance of the business. Any problems that may affect your ability to repay a loan should be raised with the lender at the earliest opportunity.

**Overdrafts**

The other primary type of debt finance is overdrafts. An overdraft facility is usually agreed upon for a fixed or twelve-month period, at the end of which the borrower must obtain the bank's agreement fee to extend the arrangement.

An overdraft may be quick and simple to arrange, and you only pay interest on the amount by which you are overdrawn. However, there are bank charges and penalties for exceeding your overdraft limit within the agreed-upon period. In addition, the bank is entitled to demand full repayment of the overdraft at very short notice that may cause a cash-flow crisis.

Overdraft finance is probably best-suited to a temporary need for working capital – for example, to cover a short-term cash shortfall.

**Matching Principle**

Use the matching principle to link your activity to the right type of financing. For a start-up or expanding business, equity finance may be the best option, especially if you are not confident that you will be able to make regular loan repayments.

For working capital, use an overdraft or factoring. For the purchasing of equipment or vehicles, used fixed-term loans, leasing, or hire purchase. For property, use a long-term mortgage.

# Grants 4

There are dozens of grants and awards available for new businesses. Your local Business Link will often be able to provide you with more information. Some of the bigger funding sources include the following:

- the National Endowment for Science
- Technology and the Arts (NESTA), which invests in small businesses that show innovation, often at a very early stage
- University Challenge Funds, supported by the Department of Trading and Industry, which invests up to £250,000 in any quality business

A grant is a financial award that can help your business develop and grow. However, grants are not easy to come by, and you'll need to put in a lot of hard work. To be in with a chance of receiving a grant, you will need to complete an application and perhaps attend an interview with the body awarding the grant.

Most grants are awarded for a specific purpose, such as buying machinery or developing a new product. Grants may also be awarded depending on your company's size, location, or prospects. The following chapter looks at the types of grants available to small and medium-sized businesses, what sort of criteria you might need to meet, and how to apply for the best chance of success.

## What Is the Difference Between a Loan and a Grant?

Grants are a source of finance for young businesses. They are awarded to help businesses develop and grow. While bank loans are given based on your ability to repay the capital, grants are generally based on what the business plans to use the capital for. Crucially, grants do not need to be repaid, unless your business fails to use the money for the agreed-upon purpose.

**A Partial Solution**

Grants are a useful source of funding, but they shouldn't be your only source. For a start, it's unlikely that a grant will cover all your business expenses. Most are highly targeted at specific projects or activities, such as buying new computer equipment or investing in new premises.

In addition, grants usually only contribute towards the cost of a project. Government grants will usually cover around 50 per cent of a project's cost, but private and research grants may cover as little as 15 per cent. Some general business grants vary according to the needs of your business – some companies may receive thousands of pounds, others only a few hundred.

It's also important to remember that grants rarely arrive in one lump sum on the day your business embarks on a new venture. Some grants are paid in fixed instalments, some when the project is finished, and some with a percentage upfront and the rest on completion. You'll need to be able to show that you have the funds necessary to complete the project, either through a loan, profits, or other investors.

## Rules and Regulations

Funding from grants can only be used for the purpose for which the grant was awarded. You cannot use a grant to meet a shortfall in another area of your business finances. This is extremely important: If you break the terms of a grant, you may well be expected to repay the money in full to the grant-awarding body.

For your own protection, keep a careful record of how you spend any grants awarded to your business. Keep receipts for any materials purchased and any other relevant paperwork.

## Can My Business Get a Grant?

Most grants are awarded to businesses based on one of three factors:

- location
- industry
- size

**Location**

A grant award based on location is available to any business within a particular geographical area. This type of grant is most common in deprived areas with high levels of unemployment where councils are keen to attract new employers. Grants may also be awarded in areas where a major industry has declined or in rural areas where it is difficult to attract skilled workers. This type of grant is often awarded by a local development agency, or councils may offer concessions on rent or rates to encourage resolution to their areas.

**Industry**

A grant awarded within a specific industry is usually designed to help boost or develop a particular sort of business. For example, there are many grants available to help companies working in agriculture and rural diversification because these sectors have suffered falling fortunes in recent years.

It's worth remembering, though, that some of these grants have special restrictions applied to them by the European commission and will be closely inspected by the commission. Grants awarded by the EC in sectors such as retail, vehicles, shipbuilding, steel, and transport may be subject to more rigorous checks than other industries.

**Size**

The vast majority of grants are only awarded to businesses of a small size – generally small or medium-sized enterprises (SNEs) employing up to 250 employees – rather than to sole traders or large companies. There are other grants available to encourage new business growth, particularly through local development agencies and councils. Your application has a greater chance of success if your project is likely to create more jobs.

## What Grants Are Available?

Check with the following entities to find out about grants that you would be eligible for:

- the government
- the European Commission
- regional development agencies (e.g. the London Development Agency)
- country enterprise boards
- local authorities, including the thirty-three London boroughs
- chambers of commerce
- universities
- charities

- private organizations

- companies

Grants are often established to fund research into new product or services. The government Link programme promotes partnerships between UK business and research organisations. A range of funding is also available through the Innovation Programme of the Department of Trade and Industry (DTI).

**Training**

The training necessary to get a grant is usually available through Business Link or Learning and Skills Council. For example, the Business Link for London adds more programmes and provides a range of free services as well as up to £1,000 pounds towards training costs.

**Entrepreneurship**

Unemployed people or those in part time or low paid jobs, between the ages of 18 and 30, can apply for funds to start a business via Prince's Trust.

**Economic Regeneration**

Business in locations designated as assisted areas may be eligible for a grant if they can prove they will stimulate regional development, contribute to urban regeneration, or improve employment prospect in the area.

**Best Practice**

The DTI offers financial support to companies seeking to make best-practice improvements to their business, such as improving manufacturing methods.

## Improving the Environment

Some grants are given for projects that reduce pollution or waste. The clean-up initiative will fund up to 75 per cent to reduce vehicle pollution.

## Grants from Europe

The Europe Commission is a source of grant funding. It's usually best to email or phone the section that deals with the particular scheme you are interested in.

For example, there are a number of European grants for companies working in the information technology and the communications industry through CORDIS, the Community Research and Development Information Service.

Other grants are awarded through schemes that offer free advice, equipment, or resources to start-ups and local businesses, rather than financial aid.

Whatever grants you apply for, don't expect instant results from your application. While you could hear from your local council within six weeks, it could be two to six months before you hear from major European grants bodies.

## How to Find Out about Grants

There are more than 2,500 grants available in the UK, so it can be hard to know where to start. Try Business Link for London's grant search. When looking to find out what grants could be available relating to your location, type of business, and purpose for seeking grants, you set a list of the relevant grants, loans, and awards.

You can also call Business Link for London for further advice and information on 08456000787. If you are a start-up or new business you will be directed to your local enterprise support organisation, which provides a range of start-up services but is not a grant provider. If you have an established business, you may be referred to a business adviser to discuss your grant funding options in more detail.

Other sources of advice on grants include banks, trade associations or professional bodies, councils, regional development agencies, and government departments.

## How to Apply for Grants

Before you apply for a grant, get the basics right. Check to make sure that your business and project matches the terms and conditions of the grant. The more closely you meet these requirements, the better chance of success you'll have.

Telephone the grant administrator directly to ensure that you have all the relevant information before you complete an application, and to confirm that you are eligible for the funding. Before you spend hours or days filling in forms and questionnaires, establish the answers to the following questions:

- Is my business eligible for funding?

- Is the grant still available, and how long will it remain available?

- When are the grants handed out? (Some schemes only pay out once a year.)

- What are the aims of the grant scheme?

- How long and what format does the application process take?

Applying for a grant can be a time-consuming process for a small company, so it's better to find out early if you're unlikely to be awarded a grant, so that you can focus your energies where you have the greatest possible chance of success.

**What Information Will I Need to Provide?**

Different grant applications take different forms, but there is certain basic information that will be required in most cases. Assembling the following information ahead of time, and making sure it is accurate and available, will save you lots of time later:

- a detailed description of your products or services

- the potential benefits of your proposed project or venture

- a plan of how the project will work, including cost

- details of relevant experience (your own and that of your key staff)

If you are applying for a large grant (more than £50,000), it's worth paying for professional advice during the application process. Many accountants or consultants are grant experts. Don't forget to negotiate on any fee paid; if you arrange a flat-rate fee, you'll still have to pay, even if your grant application is unsuccessful.

There are other things you can do to maximise your chances of winning a grant, in addition to making sure your business is eligible for a grant and your application is complete. First, make sure to submit your application before the deadline, as late entries are rarely considered. Ensure that your application meets key requirements in the most important areas: significance, approach, and innovation. Don't be afraid to make clear how much your business needs the grant – this can often be a powerful tool in winning a grants, be clear about to objective of the grant body and try to show how your proposals match those objectives and their impact on the wider community and environment.

**What Can Go Wrong?**

If your application is unsuccessful, ask the grant body why it failed so you can use that information in future proposals. The following are the most common reasons for unsuccessful grant applications:

- The project or research isn't relevant enough to the awarding body.

- The ideas or benefits of the project haven't been communicated effectively.

- The ideas in the proposal are not backed up with evidence.

- The business plan lacks clarity or direction.

- Expectations of the work involved are unrealistic.

- Impact on the wider community or industry has not been communicated efficiently.

- Information is out-of-date.

- Facilities are inadequate.

- Communication is unclear about how the funds directly contribute to the project's success or failure.

- The application fails to find funds to match the grant.

# Starting an Import or Export Business (International Trading)

**5**

If your business will involve importing or exporting goods, there are certain things you must do. For example, you must correctly declare all your imports and exports to HM Revenue and Customs (HMRC) and pay any duties along with the value-added tax (VAT) due. There are penalties for failure to comply with import and export rules and regulations.

## Importing versus Exporting

If you are importing – buying goods from outside the European Community (EC) – VAT and duty are usually charged at the point of entry to the UK. However, there may be circumstances when you could apply for relief of duty and VAT. Even if duty and VAT are payable, you may be able to defer payment.

If you are exporting – selling goods to businesses outside the UK – you may not have to charge VAT on the sale. This depends on certain conditions being met. For example, you must have official or commercial evidence that the goods have been exported from the EC. The rules for sales to EC countries differ from those for non-EC. It's important at the outset to make sure you understand what is involved.

Statistics are collected on trade between the UK and other countries. For trade with non-EC countries, these statistics are collected from the import or export declaration. For trade within the EC, they are collected from VAT returns under the Intrastat system.

HMRC can offer businesses advice and information on the following:

- import and export procedures, including simplified arrangements
- VAT, excise, and customs subjects and procedures
- VAT and duty deferment arrangements
- suspension of and relief from import charges
- refunds of duty

- how to transport goods across customs frontiers

- Intrastat and other matters concerning trade statistics

## What Is VAT?

VAT is a tax that's charged on most business transactions in the UK. Businesses add VAT to the price they charge when they provide goods and services to business customers – for example, clothing manufacturers add VAT to the prices they charge a clothes shop – and non-business customers, such as members of the public or consumers, as when a hairdressing salon includes VAT in the prices it charges members of the public.

If you're a VAT-registered business, in most cases you charge VAT on the goods and services you provide and reclaim the VAT you pay when you buy goods and services for your business. If you're not VAT-registered, you can't reclaim the VAT you pay when you purchase goods and services.

**When You Must Register for VAT**

If you're a business and the goods or services you provide count as "taxable supplies," you'll have to register for VAT if either your turnover for the previous twelve months has gone over a specific limit, called the *VAT threshold* (currently £81,000), or you think your turnover will soon go over this limit. You can choose to register for VAT if you want, even if you don't have to.

## Rates of VAT

There are different VAT rates, depending on the goods or services that are being provided. Currently there are three rates:

- standard rate – 20 per cent
- reduced rate – 5 per cent
- zero rate – 0 per cent

The standard rate of VAT is the *default rate*. This is the rate that's charged on most goods and services in the UK unless they're specifically identified as being reduced or zero-rated.

**Examples of Reduced-Rated Items**

A partial list of goods and services that may be reduced-rated, depending on the product itself and the circumstances of the sale, includes the following:

- domestic fuel and power

- installing energy-saving materials

- sanitary hygiene products

- children's car seats

**Examples of Zero-Rated Items**

A partial list of goods and services that may be zero-rated, depending on the product itself and the circumstances of the sale, includes the following:

- food, but not meals in restaurants or hot takeaways

- books and newspapers

- children's clothes and shoes

- public transport

## What Is the Tariff?

The Integrated Tariff of the United Kingdom is usually referred to as *the Tariff* and is full of information to help you with importing or exporting. It includes references to the relevant laws and regulations.

Although the UK version is called the Integrated Tariff of the United Kingdom, the same format is used throughout the EC. Importing and exporting are covered by EC regulations, so regardless of the country in which you operate, the Tariff equivalent acts as a comprehensive point of reference. Please note that all EC countries have the same commodity codes, duty rates, and procedures as the UK. The Tariff consists of three volumes:

- *Volume 1* contains essential background information for importers and exporters. It covers duty relief schemes and includes contact addresses for organizations such as the Department of Trade and Industry, Department of Environment, Food, and Rural Affairs (formerly MAFF), and the Forestry Commission. It also contains an explanation of excise duty, tariff quotas, and many similar topics.

- *Volume 2* contains the 16,000 or so commodity codes set out on a chapter-by-chapter basis. It lists duty rates and other directions, such as import licensing and preferential duty rates.

- *Volume 3* contains a box-by-box completion guide for import and export entries – the C88 form, the complete list of customs procedure codes (CPCs) for importing and exporting, the country codes for the world, lists of UK docks and airports both alphabetically and by their entry processing unit (EPU) numbers, and further general information about importing or exporting.

Tariff products are available on an annual subscription. Each December, a complete Tariff for the coming year is dispatched, followed by monthly amendments, which replace existing pages.

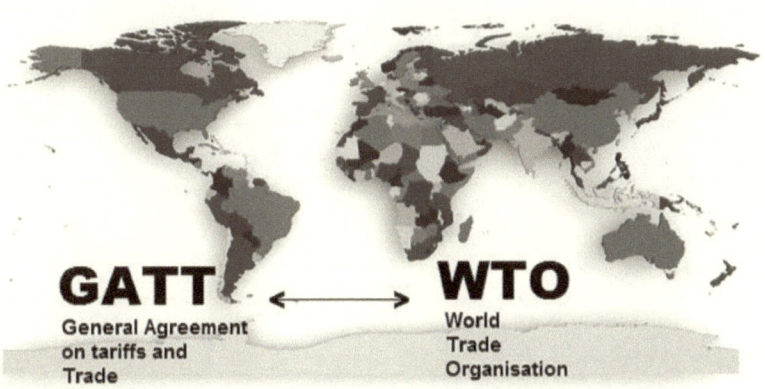

# Marketing 6

Marketing is the art of persuading people to buy goods and services. The first step in an effective marketing strategy, therefore, is understanding who your potential customers are and how to reach them. Consider the following:

- Who do I want to use my product or service?

- What makes these people buy from a particular supplier?

- What is the best way to reach them?

Answering these questions will give you a good idea of whether there is a market for your business and how to go about marketing to customers.

Advertising on local radio is great if you are marketing a business to a wide range of local people. However, if your business sells a niche product or service to people over a wide area, you may find direct mail and the Internet to be a better marketing channel.

## Sizing Up the Competition

Before you start marketing your business, it's vital to understand who else is targeting your potential customers. Look at who else customers can buy from and ask why they would choose to buy from your business instead. Can your business offer lower prices, better services, a wider range of products?

At this stage, it may be useful to conduct a SWOT analysis. This means listing all the Strengths, Weaknesses, Opportunities, and Threats faced by your new business. It can help you see clearly how your business is different from the competition and use that as the basis for any marketing materials.

## Advertising

Radio, television, and newspaper advertisements reach thousands of potential customers, but that outreach can be expensive, especially if you want to run your advertisements over a period of several weeks or months. Always negotiate for the best price before you commit.

To get the most from an advertisement, consider using a professional ad and decide what message you'd like to convey. Make sure you choose the right platform. Will a local newspaper or a specialist hobby magazine reach more potential customers?

Choose your moment carefully. Advertising is expensive, so determine when customers are most likely to buy from you. Are you selling products? If you are selling to other businesses, when do they allocate new budgets? Does advertising coincide with sales or promotions?

## Networking

In simple terms, network marketing is a network of people who have access to a range of products and services that are distributed through that network.Rather than operating via a shop front, people can buy these products and services for personal use or to sell to others. Further to this, people can assist in expanding the network by inviting others to join the network, their extending the concept to their spheres.

Over time and with more people introduced, the volume of products and services being distributed increases.

Along the way, a portion of the profits on those products and services are paid to you and people in your 'down-line'

In time the opportunity to create a regular income from a team of people using and selling products becomes a reality. Over the years, network marketing has attracted some leis than favourable perceptions. Today there are well over 20 million people around the globe involved in network marketing, also known as multi –level marketing (MLM) or direct selling, and this figure is growing, manufactures, many of them.

Fortune 300 companies, now see it as a viable and credible alternative for distributing their products and services. Reaching consumers directly through traditional retailing methods and /or outlets is not only difficult, it is extremely costly.

Today almost everything – including health supplements, cosmetics, cleaning products, training materials, clothes, cars and travel – can be and is being sold through network marketing. Some of the most famous names in the network marketing industry include – Avon, Usana, Melaleuca, Mary Kay, Quixtar, Herbalife, Amway, Tupperware, Juice Plus, Nu Skin and Aim.

Technology, especially then internet, has had a dramatic impact on the industry and more and more it is seen to be moving into the marketing mainstream.

The industry is rapidly maturing and those becoming involved in network marketing are now more often than not coming from professional backgrounds.

Network marketing has certainly come of age, it is an excellent way to get into business it has a lot of appealing aspect that cannot be found in mainstream business, and many of the 20 million people involved are making a lot many, for not a lot of work. They did then hard yards, when they started but now they enjoy the fruits of their labour with a solid passive income stream and residual

## Creating a Website

More and more business are realising the potential of the Web for extending their reach and driving revenue. Before the commercial success of the Internet, many businesses could simply not afford to market products and services on an international or even national scale. Now, for as little £10 per month, you can tell every developed nation in the world about your business.

**What Can a Website Do for Your Business?**

At the basic level, a website can be your online business card, displaying your contact details, a brief summary of the products and services you offer, and a number of examples. At the other extreme, you could create a fully enabled e-commerce solution to take payment online, process orders, and track stock levels.

What a website *can't* do is guarantee instant business success. We are now well into the online revolution, and many businesses are already on the Web and competing aggressively.

**What Do You Need for a Website?**

To create a website for your business you will need the following:

- *A domain name.* This is the address your users will type into their address bar to navigate to your website, such as www.company-name.co.uk. You can register a domain for as little as £6 per year.

- *A host.* The host is a computer much like the one you are using but without a screen, keyboard, and mouse. It is often referred to as a *server*.

- *Web authoring software.* This a software package that runs on your computer and is designed to create Web pages using, for example, HTML.

- *FTP client.* This is the bridge between your computer and your host. An FTP client is a basic program for sending your Web pages to your server so they can be viewed on the World Wide Web.

**Creating a Website on a Budget**

Most new businesses have tight budgets when it comes to marketing their brand. Fortunately, you do not need to spend a fortune to deploy a website. There are companies on the Internet that offer a simple cost-effective way to create and host a website. Basically, these companies charge you a small fee to register a domain and then provide you with access to a program that runs on their website and allows you to generate the Web pages for your site.

**Hiring a Web Consultancy**

This is typically the more expensive approach, but it often delivers the most functionality and professionalism to the end result. A Web consultancy will design and build your website to your specification. You choose the colour scheme, branding, and other features and then leave the rest to one of their Web developers.

Be sure you understand just what you're getting from a Web consultancy. Often you will still need to find a suitable hosting company and register your chosen domain name in order to publish the website.

**Doing It Yourself**

If you have the time and commitment, building your own website can be the best way to get exactly what you want from your online business without spending a fortune. Doing it yourself will teach you valuable skills you can use to update and expand your Web presence in the future.

# References and Useful Address

**British Chambers of Commerce (BCC)**

www.britishchambers.org.uk

**British Private Equity & Venture Capital Association (BVCA)**

www.bvca.co.uk

**Business Growth Fund**

www.businessgrowthfund.co.uk

**Chartered Institute of Management Accountants (CIMA)**

www.cimaglobal.com

**Confederation of British Industry (CBI)**

www.cbi.org.uk

**Department for Business Innovation & Skills**

www.gov.uk

**EEF – The Manufacturer's Organisation**

www.eef.org.uk

**Engineering and Machinery Alliance (EAMA)**

www.eama.info

**European Investment Bank (EIB)**

www.eib.org

**European Investment Fund (EIF)**

www.eif.org

**Federation of Small Business**

www.fsb.org.uk

**Finance & Leasing Association**

www.fla.org.uk

**Forum of Private Business**

www.fpb.org

**GRANTFinder**

www.grantfinder.co.uk

**HM Revenue & Customs**

www.hmrc.gov.uk

**Institute of Chartered Accountants in England & Wales (ICAEW)**

www.icaew.com

**Institute of Directors**

www.iod.com

**Prince's Youth Trust Business Fund**

www.princes-trust.org.uk

**Quoted Companies Alliances (QCA)**

www.theqca.com

**Rural Payments Agency (RPA)**

www.rpa.gov.uk

**Small Business Service**

www.smallbusiness.co.uk

**UK Business Angels Association (UKBAA)**

http://www.ukbusinessangelsassociation.org.uk

**UK Trade Info**

www.uktradeinfo.com

# NOTE

# NOTE

# NOTE

# NOTE

# NOTE

# NOTE

# NOTE

www.ingramcontent.com/pod-product-compliance
Lightning Source LLC
Chambersburg PA
CBHW030859180526
45163CB00004B/1634